SATB

15 HYMN ANTHEMS

We hope you enjoy *15 Hymn Anthems - SATB.*
Further copies are available
from your local Kevin Mayhew stockist.

In case of difficulty, please contact the publisher direct by writing to:

The Sales Department
KEVIN MAYHEW LTD
Buxhall
Stowmarket
Suffolk IP14 3BW

Phone 01449 737978
Fax 01449 737834
E-mail info@kevinmayhewltd.com

Please ask for our complete catalogue of outstanding Church Music.

First published in Great Britain in 2001 by Kevin Mayhew Ltd.

ISBN 1 84003 795 4
ISMN M 57004 915 8
Catalogue No: 1450225

0 1 2 3 4 5 6 7 8 9

Cover design by Jonathan Stroulger

Music setter: Kate Gallaher
Proof reader: Linda Ottewell

Printed and bound in Great Britain

Contents

Also available:

15 Hymn Anthems - SA Men (Catalogue No: 1450224)
15 More Hymn Anthems - SA Men (Catalogue No: 1450236)
15 More Hymn Anthems - SATB (Catalogue No: 1450235)

HAPPY ARE THEY, THEY THAT LOVE GOD

Text: Robert Bridges based on 'O quam juvat', Charles Coffin alt.
Music: June Nixon
based on the tune 'Binchester' by William Croft

21
yoke their rest.
8' + 2' mp
Man.
26
31
Sopranos
mp
2. Glad is the praise, sweet are the songs, when
36
they to - geth - er sing; and strong the

40
prayers that bow the ear of hea - ven's e -
44
ter - nal King.
S
A
T
B
p
3. Christ to their homes
49
mf
giv - eth his peace, and makes their loves his own; but ah, what
55
tares the e - vil one hath in his gar - den sown!

62
Man.

66

70
Tenors and Basses
4. Sad were our lot, e - vil this earth, did not its sor - rows
Ped.

76
cresc.
prove the path where - by the sheep may find the
cresc.

81
dim.
fold of Je - sus' love.
cresc.

86
+ Full Sw.

91
Sopranos
f
5. Then shall they know, they that love him, how hope is
All other voices
f
5. Then shall they know, they that love him, how hope is
f

96
wrought through pain, through death it -
wrought through pain, their fel - low - ship, through death it -
101
ff
allarg.
self, un - bro - ken will re - main.
ff
self, un - bro - ken will re - main.
allarg.
ff

SOUL OF MY SAVIOUR

Text: 'Anima Christi' ascribed to John XXII trans. unknown
Music: Elizabeth Hill
based on the tune 'Anima Christi' by W.J. Maher

16
wa - ter flow - ing from thy side.
20
S
A
2. Strength and pro - tec - tion may thy pas - sion be;
T
B
O
24
O bles - sed Je - sus, hear and ans - wer me;
bles - sed Je - sus, hear and ans - wer me; deep
28
deep in thy wounds, Lord, hide and shel - ter me;
in thy wounds, Lord, hide and shel - ter me; so

32
so shall I ne - ver, ne - ver part from thee.
shall I ne - ver, ne - ver part from thee.
cresc.
Ped.
Sopranos
36
f
3. Guard and de - fend me from the foe ma -
All other voices
f
f
40
lign; in death's dread mo - ments make me on - ly

44
call me,
thine; call me and bid me come to thee on
48
high, where I may praise thee with thy saints for
52
may praise thee
cresc.
S
A
aye, with thy saints for aye.
T
B cresc.
cresc.

FOR ALL THY SAINTS

Text: Richard Mant
Music: Rosalie Bonighton
based on the tune 'Mount Ephraim' by Benjamin Milgrove

Moderato leggiero (♩ = 100)

** In the choral parts the dotted rhythms should be sung with both notes slightly detached*

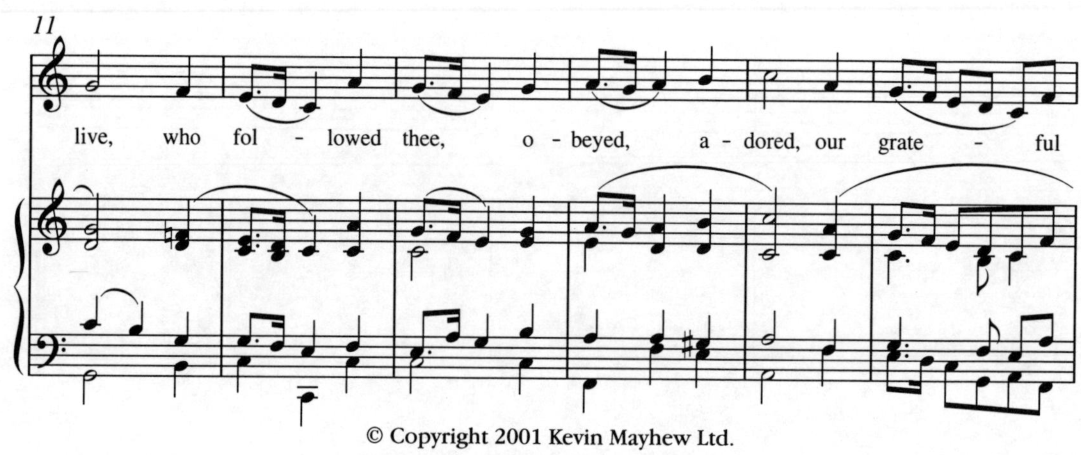

17
Tenors and Basses
For thy
hymn re - ceive.
mf 2. For all thy saints, O
Sw.
mf
Man.
Ped.
23
saints who strove in thee to die,
mp
and found a
Lord, who strove in thee to die, and found in thee a
29
S
A
T
B
full re - ward, ac - cept our thank - ful cry.
3. Thine
full re - ward, ac - cept our thank - ful cry.
mf
Man.
36
earth - ly mem - bers fit to join thy saints a -
fit, fit
fit

41
bove, in one com - mu - ni - on e - ver knit, one fel - low -
47
mp
ship of love. 4. Je - su, thy name we
mf
Gt. mp
(Man.)
53
bless, and hum - bly pray that we may fol - low them in
59
ho - li - ness, who lived and died for thee.
Sw. f
Ped.
Man.

65
f
5. All might, all praise, be thine, Fa - ther, co - e - qual
f
+ Sw. to Gt. f
Ped.
71
mf
f
Son, and Spi - rit, bond of love di - vine, while
mf
Sw.
Gt.
76
rall.
end - less a - ges run.
rall.

O FOR A CLOSER WALK WITH GOD

Text: William Cowper
Music: Stanley Vann
based on the tune 'Stracathro' by Charles Hutcheson

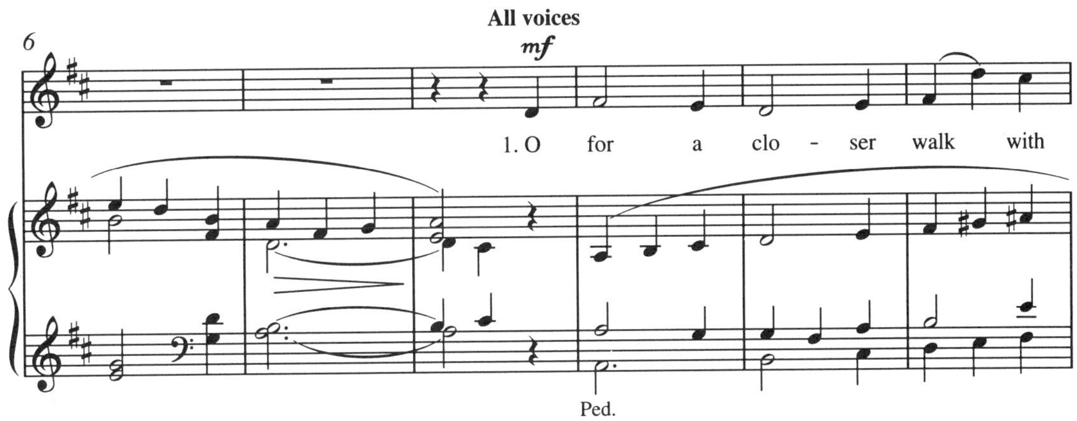

18

23
S
A
cresc.
dim.
a light to shine up - on the road that leads me
T
B
cresc.
dim.
cresc.
dim.

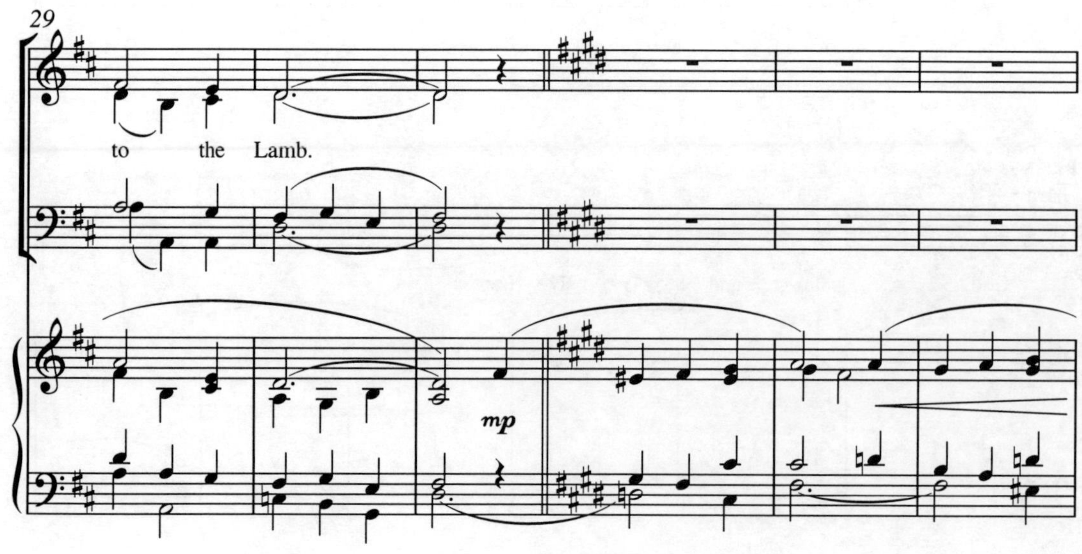
29
to the Lamb.
mp

35
Sopranos and Altos
2. What peace - ful
Man.
41
hours I once en - joyed, how sweet their mem - 'ry still!
47
mp cresc.
But they have left an ach - ing void the world can
mp cresc.
Ped.
53
Tenors and Basses
mf
ne - ver fill.
3. The dear - est i - dol I have
mf

59
cresc.
known, what - e'er that i - dol be, help me to
cresc.
65
tear it from thy throne, and wor - ship on - ly thee.
72
78
mf
S A
4. So shall my walk be close with God,
T B
mf
mf

84
cresc.
calm and se - rene my frame; so pu - rer light shall
cresc.
cresc.
90
rall.
mark the road that leads me to the
rall.
95
molto rall.
Lamb.
molto rall.

BE THOU MY VISION

Text: Irish translated by Mary Byrne and Eleanor Hull
Music: Andrew Fletcher
based on the tune 'Slane', a traditional Irish melody

17
wa - king or sleep - ing, thy pre - sence my light.
dim poco a poco
22
Sopranos
mp
2. Be thou my wis - dom, be thou my true
p
Man.
27
word, I e - ver with thee and thou with me, Lord; thou my great
33
Fa - ther, and I thy true heir; thou in me dwell - ing, and

38
I in thy care.
Ped.

44
mf
S
A
3. Be thou my breast - plate, my sword for the fight, be thou my
T
B
mf

49
ar - mour, and be thou my might, thou my soul's shel - ter, and

54
thou my high tow'r, raise thou me heav'n - ward, O Pow'r of my

59
pow'r.
mf
cresc.
Ped.
64
f
4. Rich-es I need not, nor all the world's praise, thou mine in - he - ri - tance
f
f
70
through all my days; thou, and thou on - ly, the first in my

75
mf
heart, high King of hea - ven, my trea - sure thou art!
mf
mf

80
cresc. poco a poco

84
ff
High King, when bat - tle is done, grant hea - ven's
5. High King of hea - ven, when bat - tle is done, grant hea - ven's
unis.
ff
ff

89
joy to me,
joy to me, O bright heav'n's sun; Christ of my own heart, what -

94
allarg.
fff
e - ver be - fall, still be my vi - sion, O Ru - ler of all.
fff
allarg.
fff

THE DAY THOU GAVEST, LORD, IS ENDED

Text: John Ellerton
Music: Andrew Wright
based on the tune 'St Clement' by Clement Cotterill Scholefield

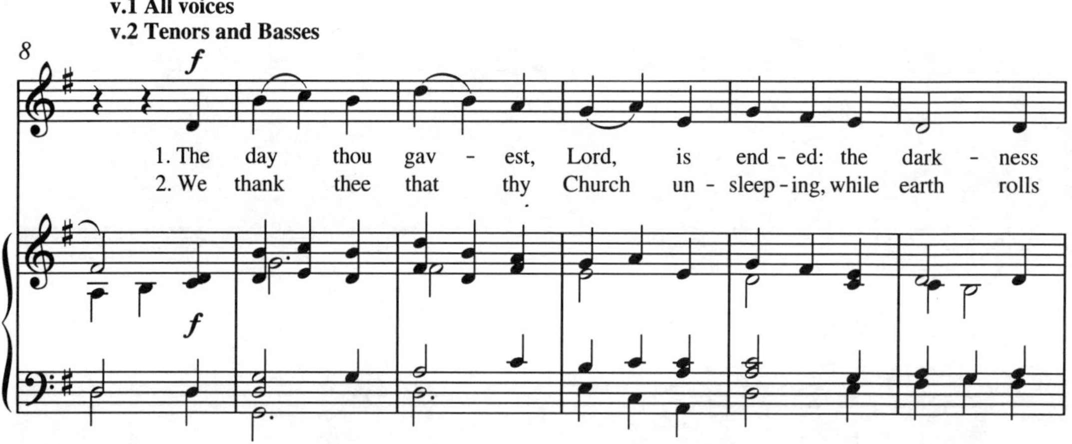

20
scend - ed; thy praise shall san - cti - fy our rest.
keep - ing, and rests not now by day or night.
25
S
A
T
B
mf
3. As o'er each con - ti -
mf
Man.
31
nent and is - land the dawn leads on a - no - ther
36
day, the voice of pray - er is ne - ver si - lent, nor

41
dies the strain of praise a - way.
45
mp
poco cresc.
Man.
Ped.
50
Oo,
mf
4. The sun that bids us rest is wa-king our
mf
mf
Oo,
55
Oo,
Oo,
breth - ren 'neath the west - ern sky, and hour by hour fresh
Oo,
Oo,

61
Oo,
lips are ma-king thy won - drous do - ings heard on high.
Oo,
f
67
Man.
Ped.
73
molto cresc.
78
Grandioso
Sopranos
più f
5. So be it, thy throne shall ne-ver, like earth's proud
All other voices
più f
5. So be it, Lord; thy throne shall ne-ver, like earth's proud
più f

84
più f
em - pires, pass a - way; thy king - dom grows for
più f
em - pires, pass a - way; thy king - dom stands, and grows for
più f

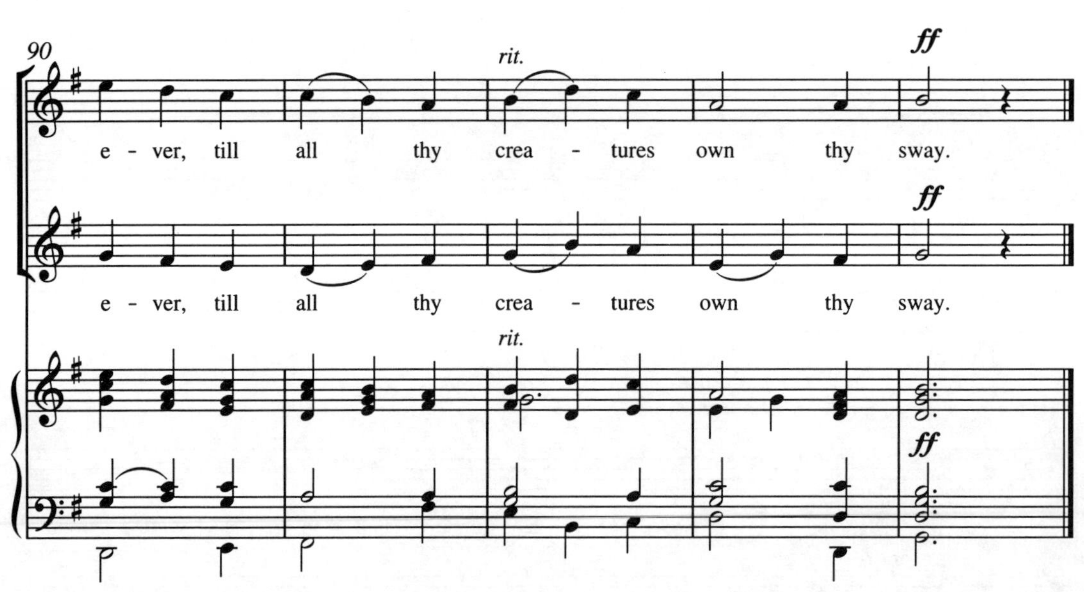
90
rit.
ff
e - ver, till all thy crea - tures own thy sway.
ff
e - ver, till all thy crea - tures own thy sway.
rit.
ff

O WORSHIP THE LORD IN THE BEAUTY OF HOLINESS

Text: John Samuel Bewley Monsell
Music: Michael Higgins
based on the tune 'Was lebet' from the 'Rheinhardt MS', Üttingen

13
claim; with gold of o - be-dience and in-cense of low - li-ness, kneel and a -
19
dore him: the Lord is his name.
mf
26
p
2. Low at his feet lay thy bur - den of care - ful-ness: high on his
p
31
heart he will bear it for thee, com - fort thy sor - rows, and

36
ans - wer thy pray'r - ful - ness, guid - ing thy steps as may best for thee be.

42
Sopranos and Altos
mp
3. Fear not to en - ter his
mp
Man.

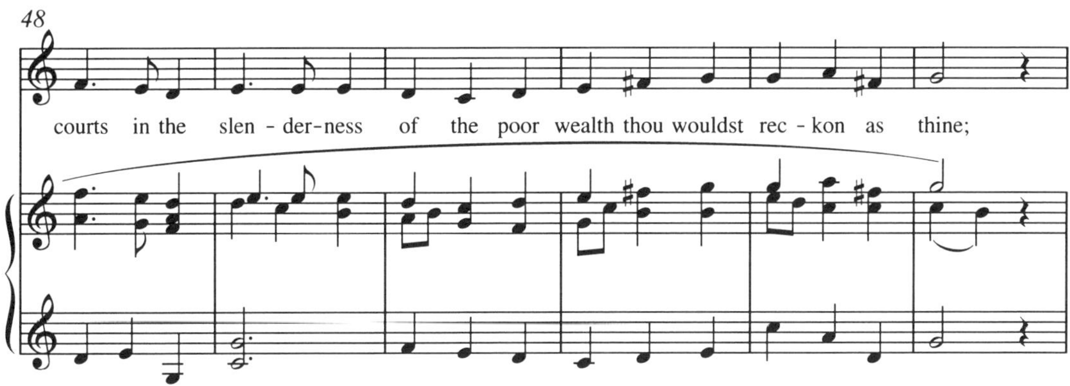

48
courts in the slen - der - ness of the poor wealth thou wouldst rec - kon as thine;

54
truth in its beau - ty, and love in its ten - der - ness, these are the

59
off - 'rings to lay on his shrine.
mf
Ped.
Tenors and Basses
65
mf
4. These, though we bring them in tremb - ling and fear - ful - ness, he will ac -
71
cept for the name that is dear; morn - ings of joy give for ev - 'nings of
77
tear - ful - ness, trust for our tremb - ling and hope for our fear.
f

All voices
f
82
O wor - ship the
Solo reed
87
Lord in the beau - ty of ho - li - ness; bow down be - fore him, his
92
glo - ry pro - claim; with gold of o - be - dience and in - cense of
97
rit.
low - li - ness, kneel and a - dore him; the Lord is his name.
rit.

GOD IS WORKING HIS PURPOSE OUT

Text: Arthur Campbell Ainger adapted by Michael Forster
Music: Andrew Moore
based on the tune 'Benson' by Millicent Kingham

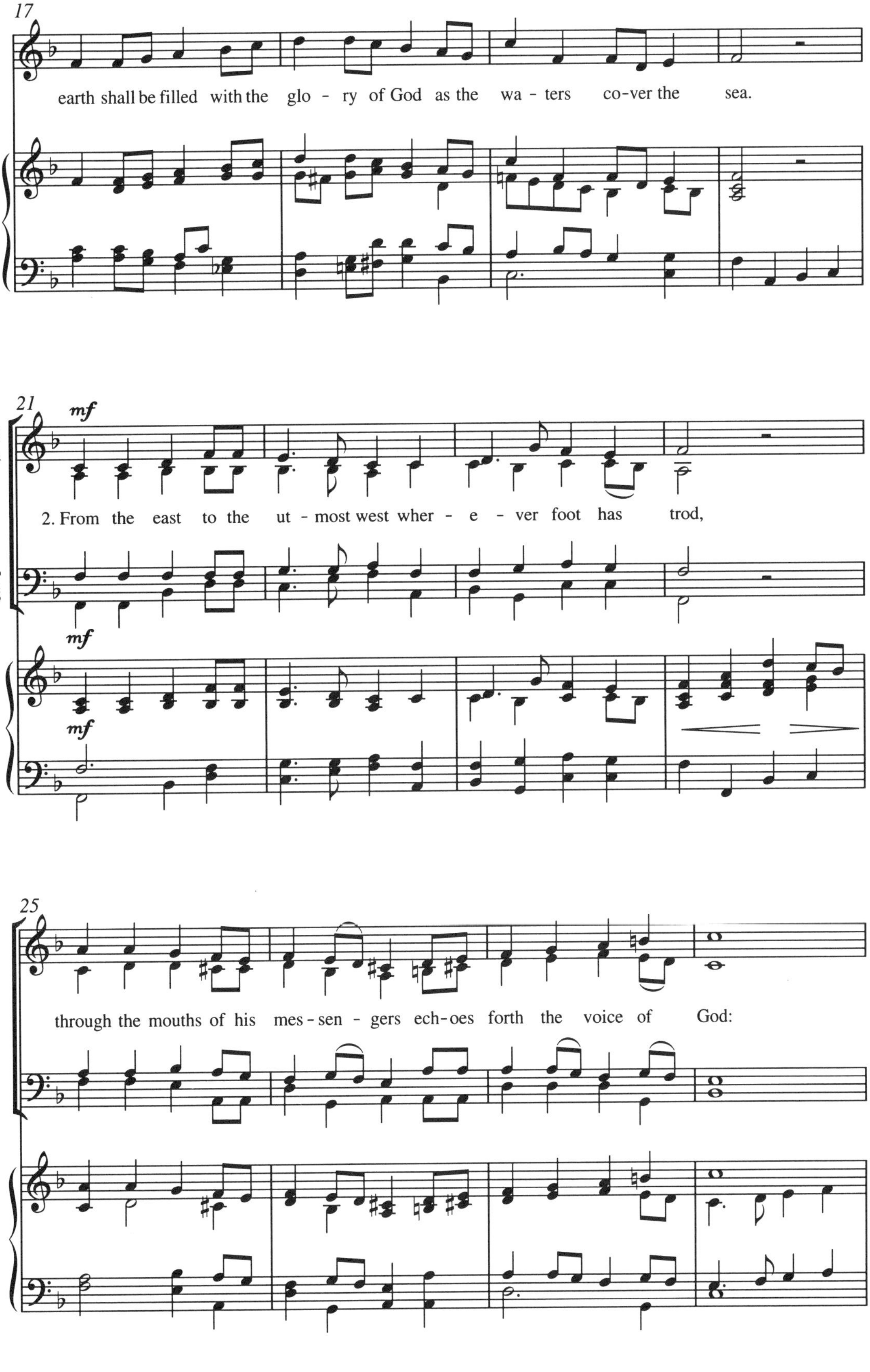

17

earth shall be filled with the glo - ry of God as the wa - ters co-ver the sea.

21

2. From the east to the ut - most west wher - e - ver foot has trod,

29
mp
cresc.
mf
'Lis - ten to me, ye con - ti - nents, ye is - lands, give ear to me, that the
mp
mf
mp
cresc.
mf
33
rall. e dim.
earth shall be filled with the glo - ry of God as the wa - ters co-ver the sea.'
rall. e dim.
mp
37
Slower
p
3. How can we do the
p
Optional accompaniment
p
Ped.

41
work of God, how pros - per and in - crease har - mo - ny in the
45
cresc.
hu - man race, and the reign of per - fect peace? What can we do to
mf
p
cresc.
49
poco a poco cresc.
urge the time, the time that shall sure - ly be, when the
poco a poco cresc.

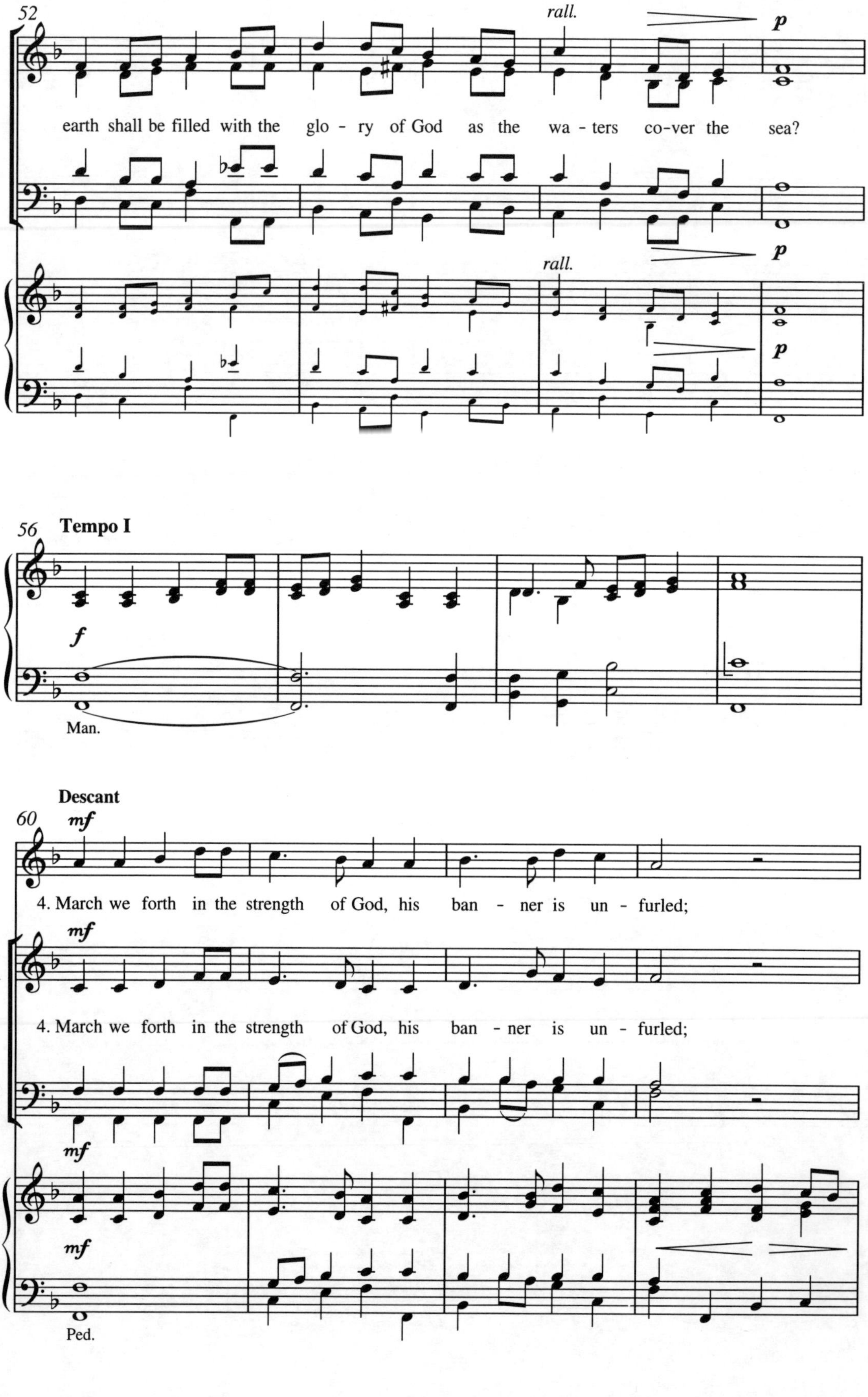

52

rall.

p

earth shall be filled with the glo - ry of God as the wa - ters co-ver the sea?

rall.

p

p

56 **Tempo I**

f

Man.

64
let the light of the gos - pel shine in the dark-ness of the world;
let the light of the gos - pel shine in the dark-ness of the world;

68
mf
strength- en the wea - ry, heal the sick and set ev-'ry cap - tive free, that the
più f
strength- en the wea - ry, heal the sick and set ev-'ry cap - tive free, that the

72
earth shall be filled with the glo - ry of God as the wa - ters co-ver the sea.
earth shall be filled with the glo - ry of God as the wa - ters co-ver the sea.

76
f
5. All our ef - forts are no - thing worth un - less God bless the deed;
f unis.
5. All our ef - forts are no - thing worth un - less God bless the deed;
f unis.
f

80
vain our hopes for the har - vest tide till he brings to life the seed.
vain our hopes for the har - vest tide till he brings to life the seed.

84
mf
più f
Yet e - ver near - er draws the time, the time that shall sure - ly be, when the
Yet e - ver near - er draws the time, the time that shall sure - ly be, when the

88
f
cresc.
rit.
ff
earth shall be filled with the glo - ry of God as the wa - ters co - ver the sea.
f
cresc.
ff
earth shall be filled with the glo - ry of God as the wa - ters co - ver the sea.
rit.
f
cresc.
ff
ff

I NEED THEE EVERY HOUR

Text: Annie Sherwood Hawks
Music: John Marsh
based on the tune by Robert Lowry

14
need thee! ev - 'ry hour I need thee; O bless me now, my Sa - viour! I
19
come to thee.
Man.
Ped. 16'
24
mf
3. I need thee ev-'ry hour, in joy or pain; come
4. I need thee ev-'ry hour; teach me thy will, and
mf
Optional accompaniment
mf

29
poco cresc.
pp
quick - ly and a - bide, or life is vain.
thy rich pro - mi - ses in me ful - fil. I
poco cresc.
pp
poco cresc.
pp
33
need thee, O I need thee! ev - 'ry hour I need thee; O
37
bless me now, my Saviour! I come to thee.

41
All voices
f
5. I need thee ev-'ry
poco cresc.
mf
Man.
Ped. 16'

46
hour, most Ho - ly One; O make me thine in - deed, thou

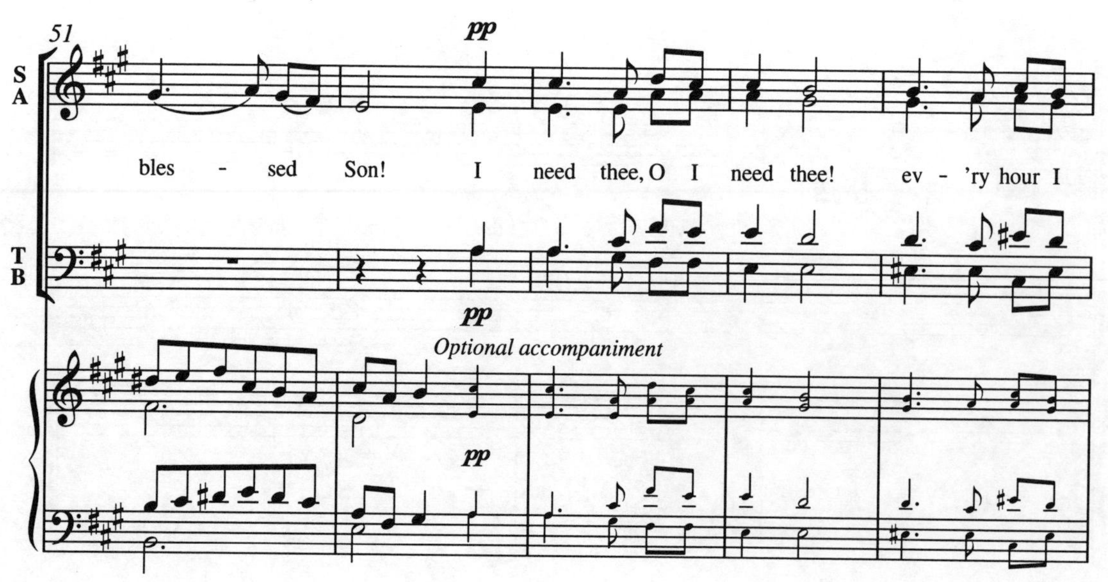
51
pp
S
A
bles - sed Son! I need thee, O I need thee! ev - 'ry hour I
T
B
pp
Optional accompaniment
pp

56
need thee; O bless me now, my Sa - viour! I come to

60
Slower
rall.
thee, I come to thee.
Slower
rall.
Sw. pp
Ped 32'

THE GOD OF ABRAHAM PRAISE

Text: Thomas Olivers based on the Hebrew 'Yigdal', alt.
Music: Andrew Wright
based on the tune 'Leoni', a traditional Hebrew melody

15
God of love; Je - ho - vah, great I Am, by earth and heav'n con -
20
fessed; we bow and bless the sa - cred name, for e - ver blest.
25
v.2 Tenors and Basses
mf
2. The God of Ab - raham praise, at
God of Ab - raham praise, whose
mf

31
whose su - preme com - mand from earth we rise, and seek the joys at his right
all - suf - fi - cient grace shall guide us all our hap - py days, in all our

36
hand: we all on earth for - sake, its wis - dom, fame and pow - er; and
ways: he is our faith - ful friend; he is our gra - cious God; and

1. v.3 Sopranos and Altos
2.
41
him our on - ly por - tion make, our shield and tow'r. 3.The
he will save us to the end through Je - sus' blood.

46
mp poco legato
4. He by him-self has sworn – we on his oath de -
mp poco legato
51
pend – we shall, on ea-gles' wings up-borne, to heav'n as - cend:
we shall as -
we
56
cend, be - hold his face, we shall his pow'r a - dore, and
cresc.
cresc.
shall be-hold his face, we shall his pow'r a - dore, and
60
sing the won-ders of his grace for e - ver - more.
f
Man.
Ped.

65
Man.
Ped.

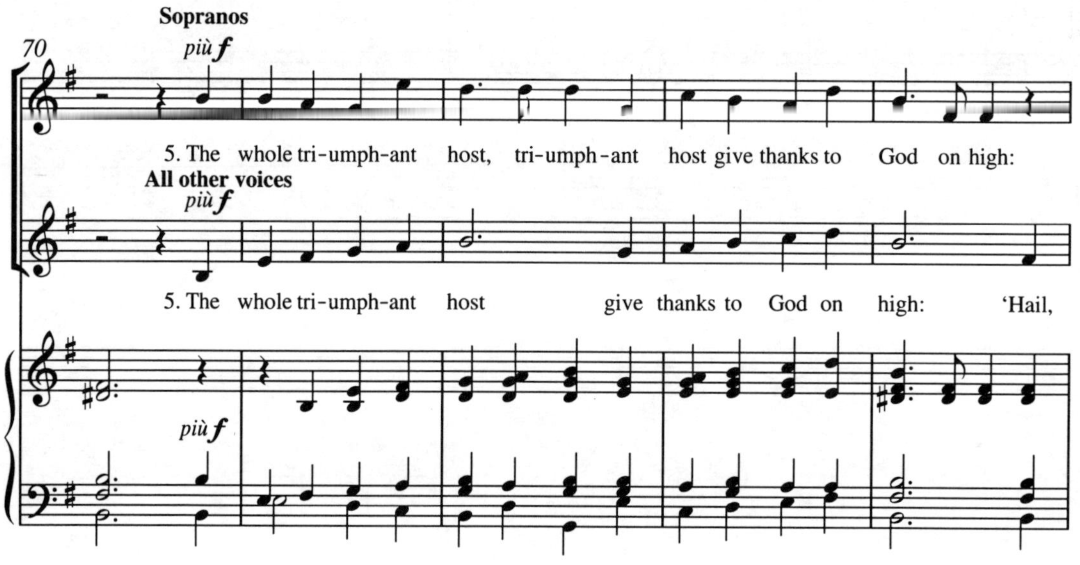
Sopranos
70
più f
5. The whole tri-umph-ant host, tri-umph-ant host give thanks to God on high:
All other voices
più f
5. The whole tri-umph-ant host give thanks to God on high: 'Hail,
più f

75
ff
'Hail, Fa - ther, Son and Ho - ly Ghost!' they e - ver cry: Hail,
ff
Fa - ther, Son and Ho - ly Ghost!' they e - ver cry: Hail
ff

79
Ab - raham's God and ours! We join the throng, and
Ab - raham's God and ours! We join the heav'n - ly throng, and
83
ce - le - brate with all our pow'rs in end - less song, we
87
molto rit.
ce - le - brate with all our pow'rs in end - less song.
molto rit.

O LOVE THAT WILT NOT LET ME GO

Text: George Matheson
Music: Robert Jones
based on the tune 'St Margaret' by Albert Lister Peace

14
cresc.
ff
in thine o-cean depths its flow may rich-er, full - er be.
cresc.
ff
cresc.
ff
Sw. mp
Man.
18
Sopranos and Altos (or Soprano solo) mp
2. O Light that fol-low'st all my way, I
22
yield my flick-'ring torch to thee; my heart re-stores its bor-rowed ray, that
26
cresc.
f
Tenors and Basses
in thy sun-shine's blaze its day may bright-er, fair - er be. 3. O
cresc.
f

30
Joy that seek-est me through pain, I can - not close my heart to thee; I
Gt. mf
Ped.
34
trace the rain-bow through the rain, and feel the pro-mise is not
37
cresc.
vain that morn shall tear - less be.
f
cresc.
f
ff
41

45
S
A
T
B
f
4. O Cross that lift - est up my head, I
f
f
Man.
48
dare not ask to fly from thee: I lay in dust life's glo - ry dead, and
Ped.
52
cresc.
rall.
ff
from the ground there blos - soms red life that shall end - less be.
cresc.
rall.
ff
cresc.
ff

For Norman Tattersall

JUST A CLOSER WALK WITH THEE

Text: Traditional
Music: Betty Roe
based on the traditional melody

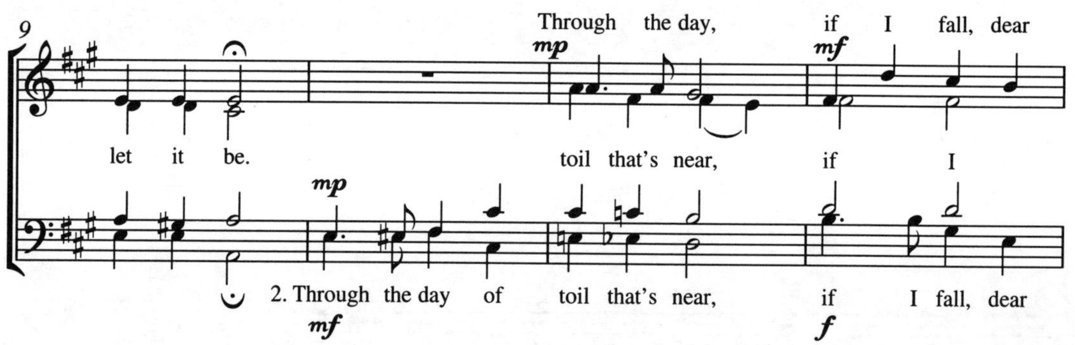

18
p
pp
None but thee, dear Lord, none but thee. 3. When my fee - ble
p
pp

23
mf
f
life is o'er, time for me will be no more. Guide me
mf
f

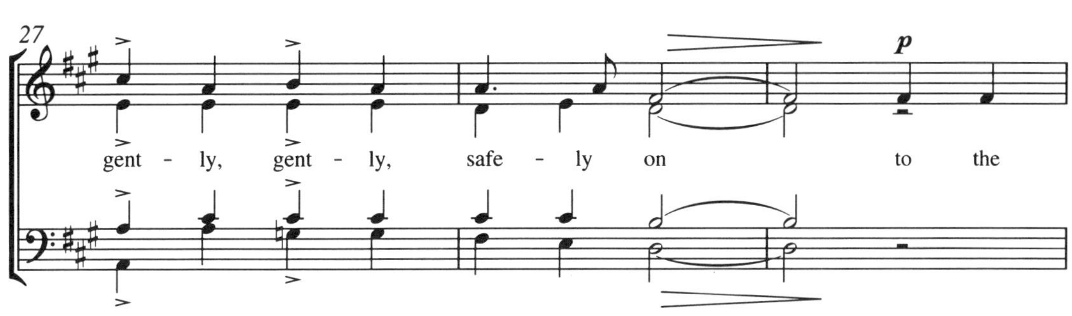
27
p
gent - ly, gent - ly, safe - ly on to the

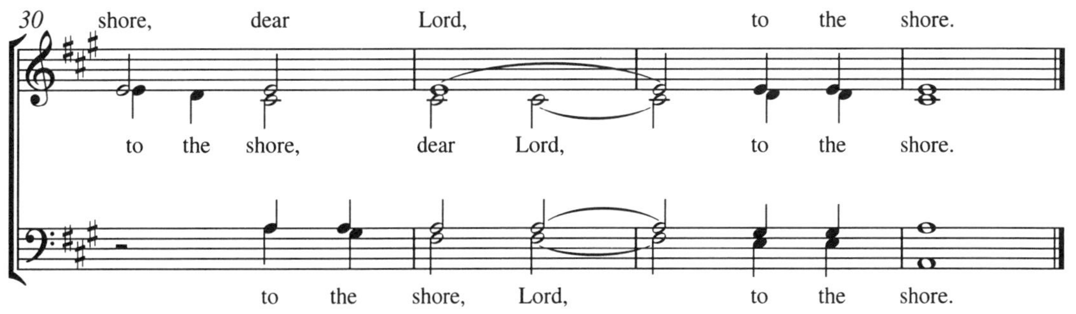
30
shore, dear Lord, to the shore.
to the shore, dear Lord, to the shore.
to the shore, Lord, to the shore.

GOD OF MERCY, GOD OF GRACE

Text: Henry Francis Lyte based on Psalm 67, alt.
Music: Andrew Fletcher
based on the tune 'Heathlands' by Henry Smart

13
f
shine up - on us, Sa - viour, shine, fill thy Church with light di - vine;
f
f
17
mf
and thy sav - ing health ex - tend un - to earth's re - mo - test end.
mf
mf
21

Tenors and Basses
25
mf
2. Let the peo - ple praise thee, Lord; be by all that live a - dored;
29
f
let the na - tions shout and sing glo - ry to their Sa - viour King;
33
mf
at thy feet their tri - bute pay, and thy ho - ly will o - bey.
37
cresc.

All voices
41
f
3. Let the peo - ple praise thee, Lord; earth shall then her fruits af - ford;
f
45
più f
God to us his bless - ing give, we to God de - vo - ted live;
più f
49
S A
ff
rall.
all be - low, and all a - bove, one in joy and light and love.
Tenors and Basses
ff
rall.
ff
53
a tempo
rall.
f

DEAR LORD AND FATHER OF MANKIND

Text: John Greenleaf Whittier
Music: Rosalie Bonighton
based on the tune 'Repton' by Charles Hubert Hastings Parry

13
mp
poco rit.
a tempo
S mf
A
praise, in deep - er rev - 'rence praise. 2. In sim - ple trust like
T
B mf
poco rit.

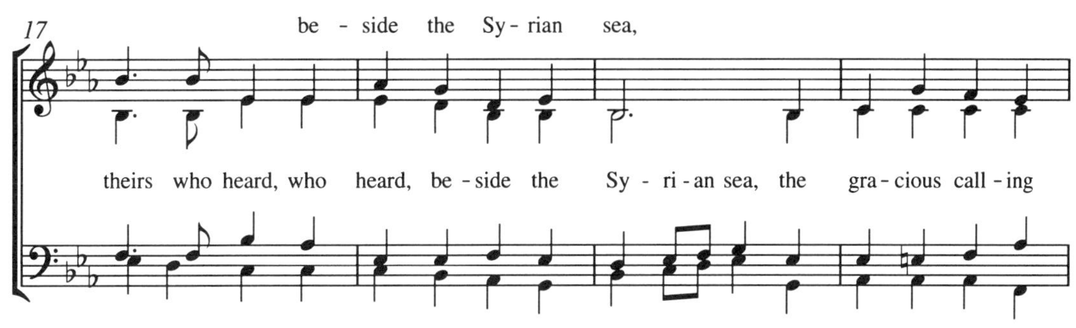
17
be - side the Sy - rian sea,
theirs who heard, who heard, be - side the Sy - ri - an sea, the gra - cious call - ing

21
of the Lord, let us, like them, with - out a word, rise up and fol - low

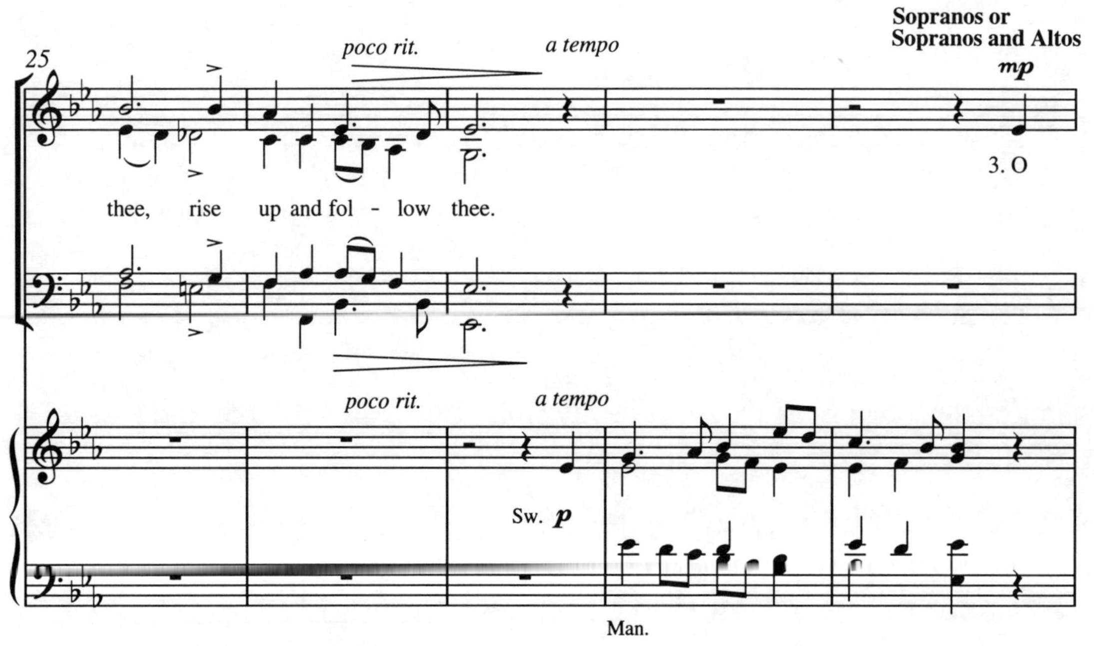
Sopranos or
Sopranos and Altos
25
poco rit.
a tempo
mp
3. O
thee, rise up and fol - low thee.
poco rit.
a tempo
Sw. p
Man.

30
Sab - bath rest by Ga - li - lee! O calm of hills a - bove, where
mp

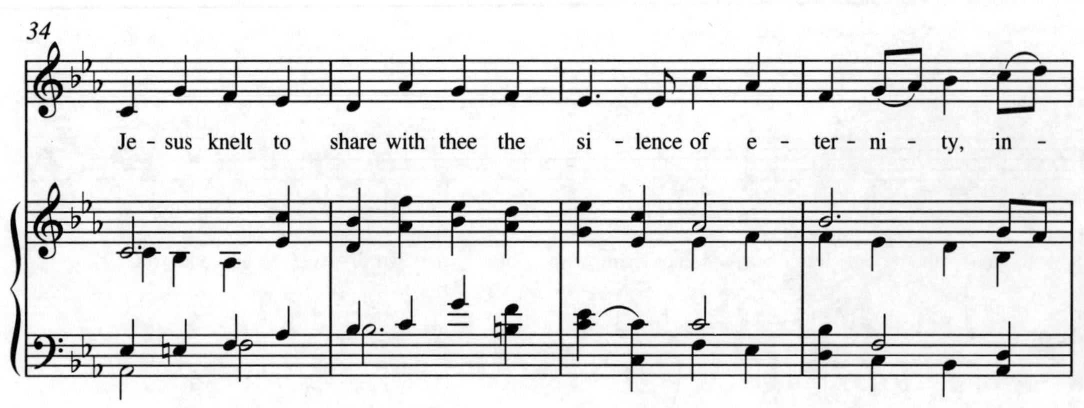
34
Je - sus knelt to share with thee the si - lence of e - ter - ni - ty, in -

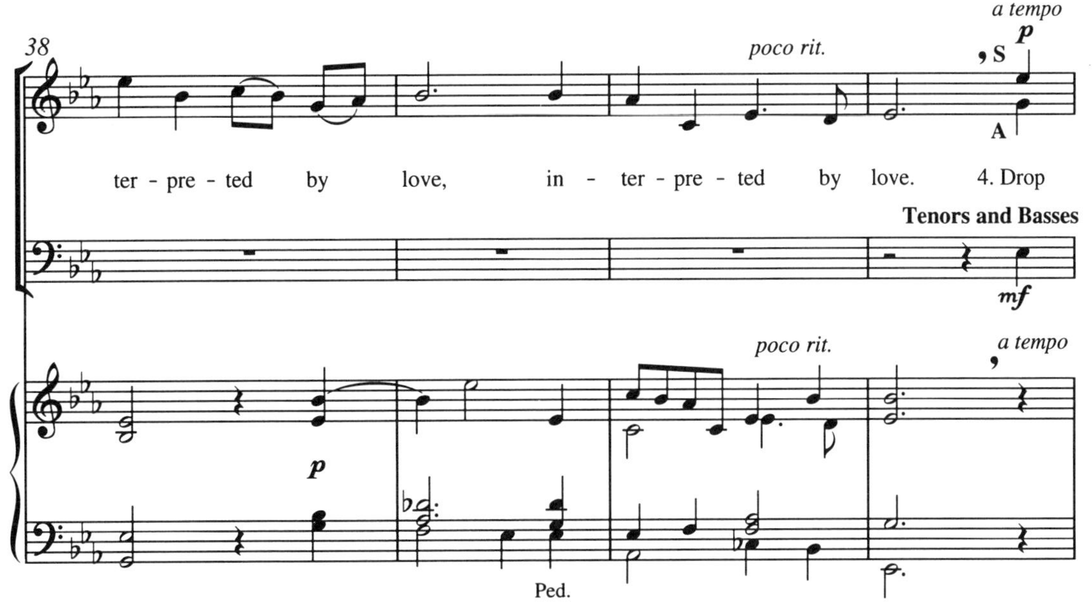
38
a tempo
poco rit.
S
A
ter - pre - ted by love, in - ter - pre - ted by love. 4. Drop
Tenors and Basses
mf
poco rit.
a tempo
p
Ped.

42
thy still dews of qui - et - ness, till all our striv - ings cease; take

46
from our souls the strain and stress, and let our ord - ered lives con - fess the

50
p
poco rit.
a tempo
beau - ty of thy peace, the beau - ty of thy peace.
mp
poco rit.
a tempo
p
Sw. mp
(Ped.)
54
mf
5. Breathe through the heats of our de - sire thy
mf
Gt. mf
58
cool - ness and thy balm; let sense be dumb, let flesh re - tire; speak

62
mp
O still small voice of
through the earth-quake, wind and fire, O still small voice of calm, O
mp
Sw. mp
poco rit.
p
66
calm, voice of calm.
rall.
still small voice of calm.
p
poco rit.
a tempo
rall.
p

MAN OF SORROWS

Text: Philipp Bliss alt.
Music: Stanley Vann
based on the tune 'Gethsemane' by Philipp Bliss

17
rall.
a tempo
f
ru - ined sin - ners to re - claim! Al - le - lu - ia! What a Sa - viour!
21
Tenors and Basses mf
2. Bear - ing shame and scoff - ing rude, in my place con -
mf
26
rall.
f a tempo
dim.
demned he stood; sealed my par - don with his blood; Al - le - lu - ia! What a Sa - viour!
31
Sopranos and Altos
p
3. Guil - ty, vile and help - less we; spot - less Lamb of

36
rall.
a tempo
God was he: full a - tone - ment - can it be? Al - le - lu - ia! What a
rall.
a tempo
40
rall.
Sa - viour!
rall.
sf
Poco adagio
All voices
45
p
rall.
pp
4. Lift - ed up was he to die: 'It is fin - ished!' was his cry;
rall.
p
Tempo I
49
f
S
A
now in heav'n ex - alt - ed high: Al - le - lu - ia! What a Sa - viour!
T
B
f
f

53
poco rall.

57
poco meno mosso
f
5. When he comes, our glo - rious King, all his ran-somed home to bring,
f
poco meno mosso
f

Maestoso
61
rall e cresc.
ff
rall.
then a - new this song we'll sing: Al - le - lu - ia! What a Sa - viour!
ff
rall e cresc.
rall.
ff